We Met Online

I Talk You Talk Press

CONTENTS

STORY 1: CLOSE TO HOME

Peter is a farmer. He lives alone. His farm is far from the city. He does not see people very often. He goes into the city once a week, to go to the supermarket. Peter is lonely. He wants a wife, and children, but he has no chance to meet anyone.

One day, he has an idea.

I often read about Internet dating in the newspaper, he thinks. *Maybe I could try it. I can't find a wife near here. But maybe I can find someone in the city.*

He looks on the Internet, and finds a dating site.

This site looks OK, he thinks. *But, maybe there are more.*

He looks again, and finds two more sites. *Which site should I choose? All of the sites say 'We can introduce you to your perfect partner!' But if I only use one site, I only have one chance. I will join all three sites. Then, I can meet three women. I have a better chance of finding my perfect partner!*

Peter joins the three dating sites. It is very easy. The sites will introduce him to some women.

Every day, Peter checks the site and his email. He is waiting for messages from the sites. He is worried.

Maybe women from the city don't want to live on a farm, he thinks. *It will be very difficult for me to find a wife.*

A few days later, one of the sites sends him an introduction to a woman. Her name is Melinda. She lives in the city. She can meet him on Friday night. The next day, the other two sites send him introductions. One of the women is Paula. She also lives in the city. She wants to meet him on Saturday. The other woman is Sandra. Sandra sends an email. She can meet him any time.

Peter replies: --- *I can meet you for lunch on Sunday. Is that OK?* ---
I can stay in the city from Friday to Sunday evening. I can have dates with all three women. Maybe one of them will like me, and I will like one of them! he thinks.

Peter reserves a hotel in the city for Friday and Saturday night. He is very nervous and excited. He cannot focus on his farm work. He is always thinking about the dates.

What should I wear? What can I talk about? Are these women looking for a husband? Or just a boyfriend? Will they want to date a farmer?

It is Friday. Peter packs a small bag of clothes and gets into his car. It will take two hours to drive to the city.

I must stop for gas at the gas station, he thinks. After driving for thirty minutes, he stops at the gas station. The woman in the gas station is very friendly. Her name is Lindy.

"Are you going into the city for anything special?" she asks.

Peter is excited. He wants to tell someone about his plan. So he tells Lindy.

"I'm going to have three dates!" he says. "I am trying Internet dating. But I am very nervous. What can I talk about with the women? If I say 'I am a farmer', maybe they won't want to date me. Maybe they are city girls."

"Just relax! And don't worry!" says Lindy. "Be natural. Tell them you are a farmer. Many women would like to live in the countryside, with its fresh air and nature. Many women feel tired living in the city. There are many cars and it is noisy. I like living in the countryside. Many other women are the same. Good luck!"

"Thank you," says Peter. "I will tell you about my dates next time I see you!"

Peter gets back into his car. He feels better after talking to Lindy.
Maybe I will find a wife this weekend, he thinks.

Peter arrives in the city and checks in to the hotel. He has a shower and puts on a pair of smart trousers and a new white shirt. He looks at himself in the mirror.

I look different, he thinks. *Usually, I wear farm clothes. But I look like a businessman! I hope Melinda likes me!*

Peter arrives at the restaurant early. It is an Italian restaurant. Melinda chose it. At 7:30, a woman with short brown hair, wearing a grey suit, comes to his table. He stands up.

"Are you Peter?" she asks.

"Yes, I am," says Peter nervously.

"I'm Melinda." She holds out her hand. Peter shakes it.

Melinda sits down. They order some food and start to talk.

"So what do you do?" asks Peter.

"I work for a large store. I'm a manager there," says Melinda.

"Do you enjoy your job?" asks Peter.

"I love my job. I am a manager now, but I hope to become a senior manager soon. My boss says, 'You will be senior manager before next year.' I am excited. If I become senior manager, I can take international business trips!"

"Oh, I see. That's nice," says Peter.

"And what do you do?" asks Melinda.

"I am a farmer," says Peter.

Melinda looks at him. "Oh," she says. "A farmer...that's...that's nice. So you live in the countryside."

"Yes, I do", says Peter.

This is not good, he thinks. *She is a career woman. She is a city girl. She won't want to live on a farm with me!*

After that, Peter and Melinda talk about the news, and the city, but they don't talk about each other. The date is not a success.

Peter goes back to his hotel. He feels a little sad.

Melinda was a nice person, but she was not a good match. Lindy said 'Relax! Many women would like to live in the countryside!' But not Melinda, thinks Peter. *But it is OK. I have two more dates!*

The next day, Peter visits some museums. Usually, he does not have the chance to spend much time in the city. He is always working hard on his farm.

Soon it is evening. It is time for his date with Paula. He plans to meet her in a wine bar at 7:30. He arrives at 7:15, but she is already there.

"Are you Paula?" he asks.

She looks at her watch. "Yes, I am. Are you Peter?"

"Yes."

"We arranged to meet at seven o'clock. You are late," she says.

"Seven? No, I think we arranged to meet at seven thirty," says Peter.

"Seven!" says Paula. Peter is surprised. She seems a little angry.

"Waiter! Waiter! Bring a bottle of red wine!" she shouts to a waiter passing the table.

"So, what do you do Peter?" asks Paula.

"I'm a farmer," he says.

"A farmer? I love the countryside! I love horses!" says Paula.

That is good, thinks Peter. *She likes the countryside. Maybe she is a good match...*

They drink the bottle of wine. Paula is becoming drunk. She is talking about herself a lot.

"So when I was young, my father took me horse-riding. We went every summer. I'm a great horse rider. And I....Waiter! Waiter! More wine! More wine!" shouts Paula.

She looks at Peter's glass. "Come on, drink! You are a slow drinker!" she says. "So, I won the horse-riding tournament in my town, and I...."

I don't think she is the right woman for me, thinks Peter. *I will try to leave early.*

Back at the hotel, Peter is feeling a little sad again. *Paula likes the countryside, and she likes horses. That was a great start! But she talked about her life too much, and she drank so much wine...she is not right for me. I will tell Lindy about her when I go to the gas station. I'm sure she will say, 'She is a bad match for you'.*

The next morning, Peter wakes up early.

That was strange, he thinks. *I had a dream. I was married. I had a wife. And that wife was Lindy! I was thinking about Lindy before I went to sleep. So she appeared in my dream. Interesting!*

On Sunday it is very sunny. Peter and Sandra have lunch. They talk a lot and Peter enjoys it very much.

Maybe she is the one! Maybe Sandra is my perfect match! he thinks. *I would like to talk to her some more.*

"It's a nice day," he says. "Shall we go for a walk in the park?"

"In the park?" she asks. "But there are insects! Bees and spiders! I don't like natural places!"

"Oh," says Peter. *She would not like the farm,* he thinks. *There are many insects on the farm. Maybe she isn't my perfect match...*

Peter gets into his car to drive back to his farm. He arrives home in the evening.

The next day, he starts to work on his farm again. All week, he thinks about the three women.

Melinda and Sandra are nice, but they don't like the countryside. Paula likes the countryside, but she is not a good person for me. What should I do? Should I try another dating site? Should I try and meet more women? Or should I just give up? I have an idea. I will ask Lindy. She gave me good advice before. Maybe she will give me good advice again.

Peter drives to the gas station. There is a man working there.

"Excuse me," says Peter. "Is Lindy working today?"

"Lindy? Oh, she quit last week."

"Pardon? She quit?" asks Peter.

"Yes, she quit. She doesn't work here anymore," says the man.

"Where did she go?" asks Peter.

"She went to the city. She wanted to get married. She wanted to stay here in this area, but she said, 'I have no chance of finding a boyfriend here'. So she moved to the city."

Peter walks out of the gas station. He is in shock. He goes home.

He cannot stop thinking about Lindy. He was thinking about Lindy when he was on his dates. He was thinking about her advice. He wanted to tell her about his dates with the women. He had a dream about her. Now he understands.

She was the perfect woman for me! he thinks. *The perfect woman for me was not in the city. She was here, close to home!*

He calls the garage. He says, "I must talk to Lindy! It's very important! Could you please call her? Could you please ask her to call Peter from the farm? My number is 012-456-890."

He waits and waits. He is very nervous, but finally, the telephone rings. It's Lindy!

Peter smiles. "Lindy, the next time I go to the city, will you go out on a date with me?" he asks.

"Of course," she says. "I was waiting for you to ask me. I only went to the city when you started dating other women!"

STORY 2: A TERRIBLE EXPERIENCE

Sue cannot believe it. Kevin is perfect. He sends her nice emails every day. Yesterday, he sent her a large bouquet of red roses with a message:

--- I am coming to see you on Friday night. ---

Sue is very excited. Kevin lives in the next city. It is two hours to the city by car, so she does not see him often.

Sue met Kevin on an online dating site last month. They have met twice.

When he comes here, we will go to a nice restaurant. Maybe we will go to watch a movie. It will be a wonderful night, thinks Sue.

Kevin arrives on Friday evening. He stays in a hotel. They go to a restaurant in the city.

"I'm so happy I found you," says Sue.

"I'm so happy I found you too," says Kevin. "I enjoy my time with you. But we meet in your hometown every time. Next time, please come to my city. You can stay at my apartment."

Sue is surprised. *Is it OK to stay at his apartment?* she thinks. *I'll think about it, and I'll ask my friends.*

Kevin goes home on Saturday afternoon. Sue calls her friend Anna.

"Anna, Kevin said, 'Please come to my city. You can stay at my apartment.' What do you think?"

Anna is surprised. "I think it is dangerous," she says. "You met him last month. You don't know him very well."

"But he is so nice!" says Sue. "He is very kind and romantic."

"I think you should wait. You don't know him!" says Anna.

"I understand, but I trust him," says Sue. "I will go to stay with him next month."

"I think it's a bad idea," says Anna. "But if you want to go, I can't stop you."

Two weeks later, Sue takes the train to the next city. Kevin is waiting for her.

He has a large bouquet of flowers.

"These are for you," he says. "Thank you for coming to stay with me. This weekend will be wonderful."

"Oh, thank you!" says Sue. "The flowers are beautiful!"

Kevin drives Sue to his apartment. He lives on the tenth floor. The apartment has views of the city.

Sue looks around. "This is a nice apartment," she says.

"Thank you," says Kevin. "I hope you like it. Tonight, I will cook a meal for you, but tomorrow, I have to work. I'm sorry."

"That's OK," says Sue.

"You can look around the city," says Kevin. "I will be home at around six pm. Then we can go to a movie."

They have a nice night. The next morning, when Sue wakes up, she sees a note next to the bed. The note says:

--- *I love you. There is fresh coffee in the pot. See you later.* ---

That is so nice, thinks Sue. She gets up and drinks the coffee. Then she has a shower and gets dressed.

I will go shopping today, she thinks. She puts her make up on, and goes to the front door. The door is locked.

How can I open the front door? she thinks. She tries to open the door, but she can't.

I should phone Kevin. He can help me. Where is my mobile phone?

Sue searches for her mobile phone, but she can't find it.

Maybe Kevin has a phone, she thinks. She searches the apartment, but there is no phone. She tries to unlock the door again, but she can't. After thirty minutes, she gives up.

She spends the day watching TV, waiting for Kevin to come home. It is a long day. Finally, at 6:00pm, she hears Kevin come home.

"Kevin! I couldn't leave the apartment!" she says. "I couldn't open the door!"

"Oh, I'm sorry!" says Kevin. "I live on my own. It is unusual for me to have visitors. I forgot! I locked the door from the outside! I'm so sorry!"

"And I can't find my phone!" says Sue.

Kevin looks in his bag. "Oh no! I took your phone! I thought it was my phone! I'm so sorry!" he says. "But I bought you some chocolates and a bottle of wine for tonight. I will cook something nice for you, and we can watch TV."

"But, you said, 'We can go to a movie,'" says Sue.

"Yes, but I'm tired. I feel like staying in the apartment tonight," says Kevin. "I really am so sorry. Please forgive me. Here, open the chocolates. They are from an expensive shop."

Sue thinks it is strange, but she says, "OK, I forgive you."

They have a nice night. Kevin is a good cook. He makes tomato sauce pasta and garlic bread, and they drink a lot of red wine.

"What shall we do tomorrow?" asks Sue.

"I'm sorry Sue, but I have to work tomorrow, too," says Kevin.

"You have to work tomorrow? But tomorrow is Sunday!" says Sue.

"I know, but it is very busy at work. I asked my boss for a holiday, but he said, 'No'. I'm so sorry."

Sue is disappointed, but she says, "It's OK. Tomorrow, I will look around the city. Please don't lock the door!"

"Of course," says Kevin. "I'm so sorry about today."

The next morning, Sue wakes up. There is fresh coffee in the pot. She drinks the coffee and gets dressed.

At 9:00am, she goes to the front door.

I don't believe this! she thinks. *The door is locked!*

She looks around the apartment for her phone. It is not there. She starts to feel scared.

Kevin locked the door again, and he took my phone, she thinks. *Something is wrong. He seems like a nice man, but he is not. I have to escape. But how can I escape?*

She hits the door loudly.

"Help! Help me!" she shouts. She waits, but no one comes.

I can try the balcony, she thinks. She goes out to the balcony.

"Help! Help me!"

There are some people on the street, but they cannot hear her.

Then, she hears the door open. She runs to the door. It is Kevin.

"What are you doing?" he shouts.

"What are you doing?" she shouts. "You locked the door again.

You took my phone again. Why?"

Kevin looks angry. "Because you are mine! You are mine now! You are going to stay here!" he shouts.

"No I'm not! Give me my phone! I'm going!"

"No you are not!" says Kevin. "You are staying here!"

Sue picks up her bag and shouts, "Give me my phone! Or I will call the police!"

"You can't call the police, because you have no phone," says Kevin laughing. "Sit down. You are staying here!"

Sue tries to run out of the apartment, but Kevin runs to the door. "You are not going," he says.

"I am!" shouts Sue. She takes a picture from the wall and throws it at Kevin. It hits his head.

"Ow! That hurt!" he shouts. She kicks his leg very hard and runs to the elevator. Luckily, the elevator is at the tenth floor. She gets in the elevator and the doors close. Kevin runs after her, but he is too late.

Sue runs out of the elevator and across the road. She stops a taxi and gets in.

"Please take me to the station," she says. "Quickly!"

The taxi driver drives very fast through the streets. They arrive at the station. Sue pays the driver and runs into the station. She buys a ticket and runs to the train.

She gets on the train. It starts to move. At last, she feels safe.

That was a terrible experience! she thinks. *I'm never going to use online dating again!*

STORY 3: I MET HER ONLINE

Harry cannot believe it. The woman sitting with him in the restaurant is very pretty. She has long brown hair and beautiful brown eyes. She is wearing a long green dress. Her name is Charlotte.

"I can't believe I met you online," says Harry. "You are so beautiful, I'm sure many men will want to date you. Why are you using online dating?"

Charlotte laughs. "It is difficult for me to find a boyfriend. I am a nurse. I usually work in the evenings, and sometimes at night. I have no time to find a boyfriend. Online dating is very easy."

Harry and Charlotte are in an expensive French restaurant in New York. Charlotte chose the restaurant.

"Shall we drink some more wine?" asks Charlotte.

Harry is a little worried. *This restaurant is expensive,* he thinks. *We have already drunk a bottle of wine. Do I have enough money?*

Charlotte is looking at him. "Are you OK?"

"Oh yes, of course, let's have another bottle," says Harry. "Here is the wine list. You choose."

I hope she chooses a cheap bottle, thinks Harry.

"Let's have this one," says Charlotte, pointing to the most expensive bottle on the list.

"Er, OK, yes, that looks good," says Harry. "But how about this one?"

He points to a cheaper one.

Charlotte looks disappointed. "I have a bottle of that in my apartment. We can drink that later."

Harry is very surprised. "Pardon?"

Charlotte smiles. "We can drink that later. When you come to my apartment."

Harry cannot believe it. *She wants me to go to her apartment later,* he thinks. *This is going to be a great night! I'm so lucky!*

"Sure. OK. Let's call the waiter," says Harry. He orders the expensive bottle of wine.

"Today is a special occasion," says Charlotte. "I have dated many men from the online dating site, but you are much better than the other men." She laughs shyly. "I like you a lot."

"I...er...I like you too," says Harry. *Is this a dream?* he thinks.

The waiter brings the wine and two glasses. They drink it. It is very good.

Harry is feeling great. "Would you like some dessert?" he asks. "Here, choose anything you like."

"Oh, thank you," says Charlotte. She looks at the dessert menu and chooses the most expensive chocolate dessert.

It's expensive, thinks Harry. *But that is OK. I am going to her apartment later!*

Harry also orders a dessert, but he orders a cheaper one. The waiter brings the desserts.

"This is wonderful," says Charlotte. "This really is a special evening. Thank you so much."

"Thank you too," says Harry. "Do you live near here?"

"Not far," says Charlotte. "We can take a taxi. You can get a taxi in the morning too."

She wants me to stay overnight! thinks Harry. *Great! I will tell all my friends tomorrow. They will be very jealous!*

It is warm in the restaurant, so Harry takes his jacket off.

"I like your blue shirt," says Charlotte. "It looks good on you."

"Oh, thank you," says Harry.

They talk about Harry's job in the bank. They drink the wine and eat their desserts.

Charlotte looks at her watch. "It's getting late. Shall we go?"

"OK," says Harry. "But I need to go to the restroom."

He goes to the restroom and looks in the mirror. He smiles. "This is your lucky night, Harry," he says. "This is your lucky night!"

When he goes back to the table, Charlotte is waiting for him.

"I'll call the waiter and pay," says Harry.

"Oh, thank you very much. I will go to the restroom," says Charlotte.

She stands up and walks away. Harry looks for his wallet in his jacket pocket.

Where is my wallet? he thinks. *I can't find my wallet.*

He looks everywhere. He looks in his jacket pockets and his pants pockets, but he cannot find his wallet. He starts to panic.

I will have to ask Charlotte to pay! This is terrible! I will wait for her to come back from the restroom and ask her. Of course, I can give her the money back tomorrow, but…oh, where is my wallet?

Ten minutes later, Harry is still waiting. Charlotte hasn't come back from the restroom. He is worried. He calls the waiter.

"Excuse me," he says.

"Yes sir?" says the waiter.

"I have a problem. I can't find my wallet, and my partner has gone to the restroom, but she hasn't returned. Have you seen her?"

"The woman in the green dress?" asks the waiter.

"Yes," says Harry.

"She didn't go to the restroom. She walked out of the front doors," says the waiter. "She is gone."

"What?" says Harry. "But…but…"

"Was she your friend?" asks the waiter.

"No, I met her online," says Harry. "Today was our first date."

"You must be careful," says the waiter. "This sometimes happens. A man meets a woman online. They meet in an expensive restaurant like this. The woman tells the man she likes him a lot. The man is pleased and excited. Then the woman leaves. With the man's wallet…"

STORY 4: A LUCKY ESCAPE

Jill is excited. She has a date tonight. She met a man on an online dating site. They have been emailing for a few weeks, but they have not exchanged photographs. Yesterday, he sent her an email. He wants to meet her. He said:

--- *Let's meet at the Green Horse pub on Central Road at 7:30 tomorrow night. I will be wearing a checked shirt and jeans.* ---

Jill reads the message again, and again.

I have a date! she thinks. She has been using online dating sites for a long time, but she rarely gets dates. Some of the men seem strange, or they want to meet her very soon. But this man seems OK. His emails are always very nice and polite.

What shall I wear? He is going to wear a checked shirt and jeans, so I should wear casual clothes too. She looks in her wardrobe. She finds a black T-shirt and jeans.

I will wear these, she thinks.

Jill is nervous, so she arrives at the pub early. She sees a man in a checked shirt and jeans sitting alone at a table.

He is already here! she thinks. *He is early too!*

She walks over to the table and sits down.

"Hi, I'm Jill," she says. "It's nice to meet you."

The man looks surprised.

"Oh, hi, Jill," he says.

They look at each other. Then the man says, "Would you like a drink, Jill?"

"Yes, a gin and tonic please," says Jill.

"Sure, just a moment," says the man. He goes to the bar.

He seems nice, thinks Jill. The man comes back.

"Here's your drink," he says.

"Thank you," says Jill. The man doesn't say anything.

"Your shirt suits you," says Jill. "Oh, thank you," says the man.

Then, they hear a noise from near the bar. There is a man in a checked shirt sitting on a bar stool. He looks angry.

"Give me a pint of beer! Now!" says the man at the bar.

"I'm serving another customer," says the barman. "Please wait."

"Now!" The man hits the bar with his hand.

"I'm serving someone else!" says the barman.

"If you don't give me a beer now, I'll get very angry!" says the man.

Jill and the man watch from the table.

"Who is that?" says the man.

"I don't know. I have never seen him before," says Jill.

"He is so rude," says the man.

"Yes, he is. I'm glad I don't know him."

And I'm glad he is not my date tonight, thinks Jill. *I'm glad my date is nice. He seems quiet and polite.*

They try to talk, but the man at the bar is very loud.

"It is difficult to talk in here," says Jill. "Shall we go somewhere else?"

The man looks very surprised.

"Somewhere else? Er, no I think here is fine," he says.

"OK," says Jill. "Can I buy you another drink?"

The man looks surprised again, but he says, "Sure. A pint of beer please."

Jill goes to the bar. The angry man has a pint of beer now, but he is still not happy. He looks at his watch many times.

"I don't believe this," he says. "I don't believe it. Where is she?"

He is waiting for a woman, thinks Jill. *Why would a woman want to meet him? He is not a nice person.*

She buys the drinks and returns to the table.

"The man is waiting for a woman," she says.

"I'm not surprised the woman hasn't come to meet him," says the man. "He is not nice."

They drink their drinks and talk about the city, and their hobbies. After about an hour, the man looks at his watch.

"I'm sorry Jill, but I must go now," he says.

"Already?" asks Jill. She is surprised.

"Yes, I am only here in the city for the weekend on business."

"Oh, I thought you lived here," says Jill. "Can I see you again?"

"You want to see me again?" asks the man. "I'm sorry, but I have a girlfriend."

The man stands up.

"You have a girlfriend?" asks Jill. She is very surprised.

"Yes, I do," says the man. "It was nice to meet you."

"But, but…wait…" says Jill.

But the man doesn't wait. He puts his coat on, smiles at Jill and walks out of the pub.

Well, that was a strange date, thinks Jill. *He had a girlfriend, so why is he using online dating?*

She finishes her drink. Then she hears the angry man at the bar. He is talking to another customer.

"I had a date tonight! I met her on a dating site! We decided to meet in here at seven thirty! But she hasn't come! That's why I'm angry!"

Jill puts her coat on quickly. *It was him!* she thinks. *He was my date! I sat with the wrong man! Or maybe he was the right man…that was a lucky escape!*

STORY 5: THE COMPANY PRESIDENT

Rebecca is a 45-year-old bank manager. She has a nice expensive apartment, and a very good job with a high salary. But she doesn't have a boyfriend.

I'd like to share my life with someone, she thinks. *Sometimes, I feel so lonely. But where can I meet someone? I want to meet someone who has a good job and a high salary too.*

She looks online, and finds a dating site for rich people with jobs with high salaries.

This site looks good, she thinks. *Maybe I will find another bank manager.*

She writes some information about herself on the dating site.

--- I am a bank manager in the city. My hobbies are travelling to other countries and art collecting. ---

After a few days, Rebecca gets a message from a man. The man says he is the president of a computer company. His name is Joseph. He lives in the same city. She looks at his photograph.

He looks nice, she thinks. She arranges a date with him.

They meet at a stylish wine bar in the city. Joseph orders the most expensive wine on the menu.

"Don't worry about the cost," he says to Rebecca. "I will pay."

They talk about their jobs, and their lives. Rebecca likes him.

"So, do you live near here?" asks Joseph.

"Yes, I live in a town house in Oak Gardens," says Rebecca.

"Oh, very nice. And your hobby is collecting art?" asks Joseph.

"Yes, I like Diego Muzsato's paintings," says Rebecca.

"Oh, he is very popular now," says Joseph. "His paintings cost a lot of money."

"Yes. He is very popular now," says Rebecca. "But I started collecting his work about ten years ago. I was very lucky. I bought some from Diego when he first started painting. I got them very cheaply. Of course I bought more later."

Joseph is interested. "So how many do you have?"

"Ten," says Rebecca.

"Ten! Ten original Diego Muzsato paintings!" says Joseph. "I hope you have a good security system!"

"Oh, yes. I have a security system. There was one in my house when I bought it. But I guess it is quite old now."

"You need a very modern security system. I will write down the name and number of the company I use."

Joseph writes down the information and gives it to Rebecca.

They talk about the paintings.

He is very interested in my life, thinks Rebecca. *I like that.*

The date is a success. Rebecca goes home and thinks about Joseph a lot.

I want to see him again, she thinks. *I'll send him a message and ask him for another date.*

Rebecca emails Joseph, but he does not reply. She calls the security company Joseph told her about. A man comes and puts in a new security system. It is expensive, but Rebecca doesn't mind. She waits a few days and sends Joseph another email. But he doesn't answer.

Maybe he doesn't want to see me again, she thinks.

She sends another email, but again, Joseph does not reply.

After a few weeks, Rebecca gives up.

One night, she goes home from work very late. She drives into her garage and walks to the front door. She goes into the house and switches on the lights.

Oh no! she thinks.

She looks around the house. She cannot believe it. Her paintings are not there.

My paintings are gone! Someone has taken my paintings!

She calls the police. The police come quickly, and check the house.

"Who did this?" says Rebecca. "Who took my paintings?"

"Have you told anyone about your art collection?" asks the policeman.

Rebecca thinks about it.

"I had a date with a man I met online. I told him about them."

"Did you use a dating site for rich people with high salaries?" asks the policeman.

"Yes, I did. Why?"

"Well, this happens a lot. You meet a man on the site, and go on a date. Then it is easy. When you are at work, they come into your house and take your things. This has happened many times in this city recently."

"So Joseph was not a real company president? He was part of a gang?" asks Rebecca.

"I think so," says the policeman.

"Joseph said 'I am the president of a computer company'. Maybe he was the president of a computer gang," says Rebecca.

"Maybe," says the policeman. "We will try to find your paintings, but I don't think there is much chance. The gangs sell things quickly."

"I can't believe this. I thought Joseph was a nice man. But he didn't email me again. I thought he wasn't interested in me," said Rebecca.

"No, he wasn't interested in you," says the policeman. "He was interested in your art collection!"

STORY 6: LET'S DANCE

"Paul, who is your date for the boss's wedding?" asks Graham.

Paul looks at Graham. "I don't know. I will probably go alone, but I don't want to go alone. But I have no girlfriend. The wedding is next month. I can't find a girlfriend in a month!"

William is sitting at the next desk. He is listening to Paul and Graham.

"I have a good idea," he says. "Look online! There are many dating sites. You can find a girlfriend very easily online."

"Online?" asks Paul. "But I think it will take time."

"Sign up to a site today. You have a month to find a girlfriend. You can find someone easily!" says Graham.

"OK, I will do that when I finish work," says Paul.

Paul works on the second floor of the company building. It is a very big company. The building has ten floors.

Now, on floor nine, Jane is worried.

The boss's wedding is soon, she thinks. *I broke up with my boyfriend last month. I am new in the office. If I go to the wedding alone, everyone will know I am single. I don't want that. I want to go to the wedding with a partner. What can I do?*

She goes to the kitchen to make a cup of coffee. *I met my last boyfriend online,* she thinks. *Maybe I can meet another man online. Maybe he can come to the boss's wedding with me.*

Later that evening, Jane logs on to the site. She looks at the profiles of some of the men. Then she sees a new profile.

This man looks OK, she thinks. *He lives in London, and is looking for a girlfriend. I'll send him a message.*

Paul is very surprised. *I signed up to the site thirty minutes ago, and already, I have a message from a woman! This is great!* he thinks.

It is Saturday night. Paul is sitting in a bar. He is waiting for the woman from the dating site.

I hope she comes, he thinks. *And I hope she looks like her photograph!*

Jane walks in. She sees Paul.

"Hi, are you Paul?" she asks.

"Yes. Are you Jane?"

"Yes, I am. Nice to meet you."

"Nice to meet you, too."

Jane buys a drink at the bar and sits down with Paul.

They talk about many things.

"Where do you work?" asks Paul.

"I work for a large company in the city," says Jane. She doesn't say the name of the company. She doesn't want to give too much personal information to Paul.

"I work for a large company too," says Paul.

They have a few more drinks, then Jane says, "It is getting late. I should go now. It was nice to meet you."

"Can I see you again?" asks Paul.

Jane smiles. "Yes, I would like that very much."

Paul is happy. His date was a success!

The next Saturday, Paul and Jane meet again in the same pub. They enjoy talking to each other very much.

Then, Paul says, "Next Saturday, I am going to a wedding. Would you like to go with me?"

"Next Saturday? I'm sorry, I can't. I am going to a wedding too," says Jane.

"That's bad luck!" says Paul. "I want to go to the wedding with someone, but I will go alone."

"I'm sorry," says Jane. "There are many weddings at this time of year."

Jane is also disappointed. She wanted to go to the wedding with Paul.

All the other women in the office will go to the wedding with their partners, but I will go alone, she thinks. *If anyone asks me about a partner, I will say he is on a business trip.*

The next day, Graham asks Paul, "So, how was your date? Is she going to the wedding with you?"

"No, I was unlucky. She is a really nice person, and I like her very much. But she is also going to a wedding on that day."

"That's too bad," says Graham. "But it is the wedding season. There are a lot of weddings at this time of year."

"Yes, Jane said that too," says Paul. "I will go to the wedding alone."

It is the day of the wedding. The wedding party is in a big hotel in the centre of London. Paul is standing talking to Graham. They are listening to the band. Some people are dancing.

"It's a big wedding party," says Graham. "Many people from the company are here. The boss invited many people!"

"Yes," says Paul. "I don't know many of the people here."

Graham is looking at a group of women standing near the buffet table.

"I think those women work in the accounting section on the ninth floor. I have seen some of them in the cafeteria a few times. I think one of the women lives near me. I sometimes see her on the train and…"

But Paul isn't listening. He is walking towards the women.

"Excuse me," he says to one of them. The woman turns around. She looks very surprised.

"Paul?"

"Jane?"

"Yes!" they say, laughing.

"I can't believe it!" says Paul.

"I can't believe it either!" says Jane.

Paul looks to the dance floor.

"Shall we dance?" asks Paul.

"Sure," says Jane. "Let's dance!"

THANK YOU

Thank you for reading We Met Online! We hope you enjoyed the story. (Word count: 6,495)

If you would like to read more graded readers, please visit our website
http://www.italkyoutalk.com

Other Level 1 graded readers include
A Business Trip to New York
A Homestay in Auckland
A Trip to London
Dear Ellen
Haruna's Story Part 1
Haruna's Story Part 2
Haruna's Story Part 3
Ken's Story Part 1
Ken's Story Part 2
Life is Surprising!
Strange Stories
The Christmas Present
The Old Hospital

ABOUT THE AUTHOR

I Talk You Talk Press is a Japan-based publisher of language textbooks, graded readers and language learning/teaching resources.

Our team is made up of highly experienced language teachers and translators, who have all studied at least one additional language to an advanced level.

This experience enables us to design our materials from the perspective of both the teacher and the learner. We consult with both teachers and language learners when designing our textbooks and graded readers, and test our materials extensively in the classroom before publication.

We are a fast-growing press, and currently publish graded readers for learners of English. We publish new graded readers monthly.

www.ingramcontent.com/pod-product-compliance
Lightning Source LLC
Chambersburg PA
CBHW022352040426
42449CB00006B/847